exhales

exhales

poems by
Brian Selkirk

Winner of the 2017
Edna Meudt Memorial Award

National Federation of State Poetry Societies, Inc.
NFSPS Press

Published May 2017
The National Federation of State Poetry Societies, Inc.
NFSPS Press
www.nfsps.com

Edit and design by Kathy Lohrum Cotton
Cover art, *Dusk On Helen's Dome*, by Natalie Johnson

Printed in the United States of America
CreateSpace, Charleston, South Carolina

ISBN-13: 978-1545590720
ISBN-10: 1545590729

For Christina Ziembo
the kindest, most generous
and compassionate person
I have ever known

and

for Joshua Sauvie
my English instructor
for always telling me to "go"

CONTENTS

In addition to his neuroscience major and psychology minor at the University of Arizona, junior Brian Selkirk is a student with interests as diverse as poetry, work, fashion, intelligence, trends, and thought. The ten-poem manuscript which won him the 2017 Meudt Award travels comfortably from Greek mythology to Hinduism's Shiva; from the island of Lesbos to the Sierra wilderness; from the surface, deep into the poet. He speaks to us variously in vocabularies of wisdom and longing and ecstasy, with smatterings of Latin, and even a title with the Korean glyph for flower, (꽃).

Selkirk is singularly creative. Contest judge Larry Woiwode notes that "the voice is its own, like no other…so clearly and distinctively original that hardly a line slips out of the timbre and cadence…."

The College Undergraduate Poetry Contest committee of the National Federation of State Poetry Societies is pleased to present Brian Selkirk's debut collection, *Exhales*: a winner indeed.

Kathy Cotton, Editor
May 2017

ACKNOWLEDGMENTS

I would like to acknowledge:

Harold Bloom, the famous literary critic, for being invaluable to the expansion of my literary consciousness.

Aleister Crowley, for being pivotal generally to my spiritual and intellectual life.

Friedrich Nietzsche, for the inestimable gift of his *Zarathustra*.

The Romantics, for giving me the vocabulary of ecstasy.

Jorge Luis Borges and Walt Whitman, for making me start over again.

J.R.R. Tolkien, for awakening my reverence for nature.

Wilhelm Reich, for providing me with a systematic, scientific apparatus for examining the soul, which enabled me to understand Jung and the rest of them.

And the NFSPS/CUP for the honor of these laurels.

Brian Selkirk

I

Magna Quies in Magna Spe
In Great Repose There Is Great Hope
or
The Last Dusk before Desertion

There are no more hours or seconds, time
is no more. No more conflict. No more friends.
There is only the East at midnight.
There are only the songs of birds, everywhere.
There are only my hands, my strength, my goodness,
my wholesomeness, my chest, my flower-scented skin.
There is only movement supervening stillness.
There is only light; even darkness is light.
There is eating and tasting and nourishment.
There is only listening.
There is the empty, erotic East, in summer, at night,
full of potential, full and taut and empty
like a skin-drum! The East slowly drums
without waking the hill-sheep, blue in the night,
without melting the April snow
or distracting the reader of ancient books
with cold intimations of nothingness.
There is only the edge of the world
with great stones and birds and waves and wind.
There is only what is behind and now.
There is death. There is the next life.
There is no time, no friends, no conflict.
There are only bird songs; the rush of waves; the throb
of the West.

II

Spring in Naples

When I am alone in meditation,
upon the book of which I turned the final leaf,
my consciousness *in toto coelo*,
and, taking to the fields, my feet are bare,
remove my shirt to cloy my skin
with wind and golden sunshine,
the youth I sense escaping me
flamboyant on my features now,
my dancing hair a flame of raven feathers,
the earth, a flame of green–
I would that universal force that set me here
would exempt me, in this moment, as Enoch,
and bring an end to endings and beginnings.
Naked, I am dressed for my hereafter–
to go admonishes this unknowable day
and the igneous voice of my golden soul–
to go this poignant impulse knows
not where; to brace, to watch, prepare,
to stride in this blinding bright travail
and leave my shoulders naked
as the sun!

III

Ama Et Fac Quod Vis
Love, and Do What You Will, *a Sonnet*

What is chastity but freedom purified,
but license with a virgin mind,
when I hang my weakness like wet towels
out to dry? No abstract jurisprudence,
no guilt, no buttoned-up sententious
condemnation. It is duty to my need
and sparing Magdalene from stoning
at the hands of the Old Testament.
What is innocence but nonresistance?
My urge need not be checked nor denied,
virtue is nothing but nature perfected,
so what is peace but a protest
against the divisiveness of ugliness
that keeps the flower of the body closed?

IV

Ode to the Unknown Muse

Sappho spread the artifice of language at your feet,
Erato.
A tapestry invented just for you.
As gentle on your naked feet as leopard skin,
man stands and woman lies upon it.
You dipped it in a deep cistern of blood.
Like the deities of erotism raised in rock
at Konarak and Khajuraho,
your strophes are tantric sculptures, are stains,
love embodied, perversity preserved.
Erato is a manifold, the jujube that lingers on
the edges of the teeth, the tension of nubility,
the butterfly of Helen's lambent legs, the rouge.
      She is the martyr who remains after the moon
         has set, wearing ankle bells, surfeiting herself
      with the dawn and the glossy exhibition of its light.
            While her eight chaste sisters shrink into
         tinsel and feathers as white as their chitons,
Erato reposes dishabille beneath the pavilion of day
        hiding like an ember in the shadows,
      singing paeans of unity and pleasure,
alone on the island of Lesbos.

V

Wherever I Am

Are not sunbeams worthy of the roots of your hair
That likewise stewards the garden of my soul;
For it radiates auburn in the shadows where you comb it
With your fingers.
Stand up from the matted grass beneath the tree
And let the sun, consuming your hair,
Doubly warm and grow my inner luxury.
Are not gales that, native to the hills,
Are ageless, Druid draughts of ageless youth,
Worthy of your skin and of your face–
Your lineament a dittany blossoming?
Are not lawns obsessed with dew that feet
Have never pressed, worthy of your supine crown
Where over you bending the monism draws a sigh?
I cannot tell, but if they're not, then how,
Will or could, I ever be, who am but one
Of your many idolaters?

VI

Fall into a Sleep and Maybe See the Sky

After the purgative night
With purple horizons and white stars,
I slept and awoke in a calm glare
Of vibrant sunlight and snow
Crisp as styrofoam.
A song was on my chest
Like the faint prick of sublimity
Although it had no words
And nothing definite to eulogize.
Just three or four notes,
A windy, plangent harmony,
Like one vast and voiceless thought.

VII

Fangs That Bite in Solitude

No, just an echo from the chasm of my solitude,
not my reified soul, or the deity of love
and magnanimity saying "Love you, I love you,
drink it from my cupped palms–my love,
like it were a distillation of the minerals
from the mountain."
I would lap it, and my tears would fill
the bowl again.
Instead, it is my own moaning at nothing
impotent to become clothed, wonder
turning cynical, the vastness it'd take love's wrist
to mitigate. Ask to hear me speak
and I would cry again, and not know why.
The seeming susurration of a gown
would turn me out from my hands to look
though only my own voice automatically rings back
in the empty air, and I blanch,
and puke. "Soul?" I but hear the "soul?" come back
with fear, its eulogies and raptures
set away; "love?" I ask the sweeping sound
the pines make, indifferent as the stars.
"Love?" comes back incredulous.
I burned my oil! "I burned my oil!"
it says back. "I know."
And there's no longer light to see the ground.

VIII

kkoch (꽃)
Flower

One morning, in the mossy backwoods
of the wilderness, gazing
out from this desolate rock on a mountaintop
at the unending horizons, hirsute, filthy,
my fingers stained black with dirt–
the faint booming of an engine
will interrupt the hungry silence, and
five miles up, I'll see the shining plane you
boarded, a glinting speck, trailing a white luster
streak East across the heaven-rock.
You're probably as prim and clean
as an origami swan, somehow foreign
to my reckoning, looking out your window
on the Sierras one last time, and seeing
the bowl-moon go down, and relishing the nostalgia
of a soft-drink you no longer believe in.
"I'll have to ask for her address," I think
out loud, "so I can send her my earlobe."

Bars of the dawn-sun fall on your lips,
your nose, your collar, your red hair.
Before you drop like a leaf in the autumn
in Virginia, where school, cobblestone
and coffee wait for you–a scarf,
perhaps, and high heels, womanly fragrances

and a lesbian–our lips will share one
final synchrony, when, out of coincidence,
my eyes up and your eyes down, we both
mutter to ourselves "goodbye."
  "Goodbye," we say, and time as laconic as sleep
will wave on unbroken in glowings and eclipsings.

IX

Why, Even If It Is a Dance, It Is for You

Mother sips her honey tea at the table
on the lawn amid the blossoms.
And her mother talks and sings and cries
over pirouetting in the kitchen as a girl,
a blithe and fumbling artist with a voluminous nimbus
of golden hair.

An evening like pink incarnadine flickers in the branches.
They hold each other's hand against the flux,
with all their children gone.
"All of life is pain," they nod,
as the elder sets her crucifix on her napkin.

She grasps her mother's hand the more remembering her age.
Life appoints death to be
the final button loosed to drop the gown
before the bed,
and again the coffins are interred
like seeds to flower as the freshest pair of eyes,
after one last kiss
and one last brush of the hand
and like a geyser of color the next generation
assumes the mantle of mortality
and passes away like a summer wind over a field
into the bed of their spouses
and in the bed of their children's memories.

It is a silence that swaddles the whole moment
when the goose bumps stand painfully on her legs

and the falling motion of all things unraveling
among the galaxies and among the clouds
and the amphibians in the puddles
are in the instant and in one abode
that draws always away in the flux,
through the impotence of the grasping hand.

With every footfall, the virgin grandchild
chasing the dog outgrows all her vestures,
which fall like leaves across the yard,
until the heresies of motion close her daughter's eyes
in grief and resume in long, peremptory silences.

Their voices ring back
from the chambers of memory like the music
of virgin dreams, fainting in the church of feelings
where our hands would envelope their faces
and their words would grope our souls.

She thumbs the widow's wedding ring
as a wasp flits about her spoon.
The West blows one final blast of scarlet
behind flickering, black leaves.

X

Shiva, an Elegy

In the wake of my tread all form is unbuilt,
Or ever the swan-song invites me.
The denouement pipes in the flute by the river
"Farewell, farewell, to the waters."

Ages of the mind, and ages of the earth,
And ages in the potter of Life,
Wrought music and singing in the domes of the forest.
"Farewell, farewell, to the drums."

My sojourn a leaf, the last leaf of autumn,
One leaf among many–the last.
The pages are dust, the river has dried,
And the wake of my tread is the last.
"Farewell, farewell, to the lie."

The pure sun of August, the gold shaven grass,
The prophetic wind in the field,
The vegetable odor of the forest at night–fear not!
The wake of my tread is the last.
"Farewell, farewell, to the path."

In the wake of my tread all form is unbuilt,
"Farewell, farewell, to the rest;
Farewell, farewell, to the last."

As a junior at the University of Arizona in Tucson, Brian Selkirk became the 2017 winner of the NFSPS College Undergraduate Poetry Edna Meudt Memorial Award for his manuscript, "Exhales." In both 2015 and 2016 he also won first place in the Sharon Naughton Student Writing Contest for Poetry at Mott Community College in Flint, Michigan.

Selkirk, a Michigan native, remembers that he began writing at the age of nine or so, when he and his family lived on a sheep farm near Gladstone, a small city tucked inside the Little Bay de Noc on the southern coast of the Upper Peninsula, and then more decisively at the age of nineteen, with the intervening years having no such interest and no ambition. He relates that what prompted his second taking up of the pen was a sense of mysticism, urgency, and romance—a quest for experience and the unlived life.

His current writing goals, which he insists remain fluid, include the working out of universal conceptions of poetry that seek to restore to readers a sense of the serious, and to continue writing essays, which he may consolidate into a book.

Larry Woiwode, Poet Laureate of North Dakota, is Writer in Residence at the University of Jamestown, where he teaches creative writing, world literature, contemporary American fiction, and Native American literature. He is the author of the poetry collection *Even Tide* (FSG, 1977) and a chapbook, *Land of Sunlit Ice* (NDSU Press, 2016). His poetry has appeared in *The Atlantic Magazine, Harpers, The New Yorker, Transatlantic Review,* etc., and is reprinted in a dozen anthologies.

His novels include *Beyond the Bedroom Wall,* finalist for the National Book Award and Book Critics Circle Award, and six of his books have been selected as "notable books of the year" by the *New York Times Book Review.* His stories appear in four volumes of *Best American Short Stories,* and he has published two memoirs, two collections of essays, a commentary on the book of Acts, and a children's book, among others.

Edna Meudt Memorial Award
Exhales by Brian Selkirk
University of Arizona, Tucson, AZ

Florence Kahn Memorial Award
A Natural Cacophony by Sydney Lo
Brown University, Providence, RI

1st Honorable Mention
"My Branch of Theology" by Seth Danleya
Corban University, Salem, OR

2nd Honorable Mention
"Revolution" by Juliana Chang
Stanford University, Palo Alto, CA

3rd Honorable Mention
"In Winter" by Grace Carhart
Gordon College, Wenham, MA

4th Honorable Mention
"8th Grade Notebook" by Alyssia Mingo
Minnesota State University, Moorhead, MN

5th Honorable Mention (Tie)

"I have no understanding of the modern world;
and I don't understand anything else"
by Caleb Rosenthal
Lawrence University, Appleton, WI

"She Wonders" by Faith King
University of Wisconsin, Superior, WI

In 1988 NFSPS planned the addition of a college-level scholarship, subsequently named in memory of NFSPS charter member and past president Edna Meudt. In 1999, with a generous bequest by Florence Kahn, the NFSPS Scholarship Award expanded to include a second competition for the Florence Kahn Memorial Award.

Now named the College Undergraduate Poetry (CUP) Competition, the annual contest is open to students working toward a degree in an accredited U.S. college or university. Winners of the Meudt and Kahn awards each receive $500, publication and 75 free copies of their chapbook, a $300 travel stipend to attend and read at the NFSPS convention, and other perks.

Contest guidelines and submission dates are posted on the NFSPS website, www.nfsps.com.

NFSPS CUP Committee:

Chair, Shirley Blackwell, New Mexico
Editor, Kathy Cotton, Illinois

The National Federation of State Poetry Societies (NFSPS) is a nonprofit organization, exclusively educational and literary. NFSPS offers linguistic and professional contexts that appeal to the mind and spirit and is dedicated to the furtherance of poetry on the national level and to uniting poets in the bonds of fellowship and understanding.

Membership in NFSPS is provided to members of any affiliated state poetry society (see www.nfsps.com). Poets in states without an affiliated society may join state societies as at-large members.

Poetry competitions sponsored by NFSPS include:
- 50 annual poetry contests with cash prizes totaling more than $6,000, including a grand prize of $1,000.

- Stevens Poetry Manuscript Competition for a full-length poetry collection.

- College Undergraduate Poetry Competition with the Florence Kahn Memorial and the Edna Meudt Memorial awards going to the top two chapbook manuscript winners.

- Manningham Trust Student Poetry Contest for winners advancing from state-level competitions.

- The BlackBerry Peach Awards for Poetry Spoken and Heard Contest for print and spoken-word poetry.

For more information on contests or membership, visit the website, www.nfsps.com.

Made in the USA
Monee, IL
07 September 2021